# MOLINEUX

# MOLINEUX
## 300 YEARS

### ALEC BREW

FONTHILL

Fonthill Media Language Policy

Fonthill Media publishes in the international English language market. One language edition is published worldwide. As there are minor differences in spelling and presentation, especially with regard to American English and British English, a policy is necessary to define which form of English to use. The Fonthill Policy is to use the form of English native to the author. Alec Brew was born and educated in England; therefore British English has been adopted in this publication.

Fonthill Media Limited
Fonthill Media LLC
www.fonthillmedia.com
office@fonthillmedia.com

First published in the United Kingdom and the United States of America 2019

British Library Cataloguing in Publication Data:
A catalogue record for this book is available from the British Library

Typeset in 10pt on 13pt Sabon
Printed and bound in England

# Acknowledgements

I have to thank the former Wolves historian Graham Hughes for many of the photographs in this book and much of the information. A familiar sight around the ground for many years, Graham had the honour of having a stand named after him when the team were first promoted to the Premier League, a temporary stand in the corner next to Molineux Alley. Billy Howe provided me with lots of photographs of the streets around the Molineux, about which he knows most everything there is to know. In addition, I seem to have half a shelf of excellent books about the Wolves, acquired over the years from Stan Cullis' autobiography onwards. I have dipped into many of these for information as I wrote, in particular Tony Matthews' *The Wolves Encyclopaedia* and his *A-Z of Wolves*, compiled with John Hendley and Les Smith; Patrick Quirke's *History of Molineux House*; and David Dungar's recent splendid work *Cometh Light: Wolverhampton 1888–1939*. I can recommend them all. I also have to thank my parents for first taking me to a match as a babe in arms in 1947, and starting a lifelong gold and black obsession, though the first match I actually remember was in 1959 when Wolves beat Preston 3:1, and just like the tune played when they ran onto the pitch, I became a Happy Wanderer.

# Contents

Molineux Hotel at its zenith in the 1930s, with cars filling the car park then at the front.

Molineux Stadium in 2018, with Molineux House at the lower right.

# Introduction

The name Molineux is famously known throughout the world as the home of the Wolverhampton Wanderers football club. Just like Anfield, the Nou Camp, the Bernabeu, and the San Siro, Molineux Stadium is uniquely associated with the city in which it lies, and yet it is so much more than just a football ground. The name was first given to the Wolverhampton home of the Molineux family in the eighteenth century, and 130 years later, it became a hotel and its gardens the home of many entertainments and exhibitions before the local football club decided to build its stadium there.

The name came with the Normans from France, originating at Molineaux-sur-Seine near Rouen. Members of the Molyneux family, to give it one of its other spellings, were given lands in England by William the Conqueror as a reward for helping his invasion, and one large branch of the family settled in Wolverhampton, embedding the name of Molineux in the fabric of the town.

Yet it might have been so different. The house was built by a local man named John Rotton, only passing it to the Molineux family to settle a debt. How different things might have been if the name Rotton had stuck to the property, though it might have been all too appropriate in the 1980s, as the house fell into dereliction and then suffered a fire, and the stadium was in little better shape, with two sides condemned and closed and the football team plummeting to the very depths, almost to extinction. A Rotton House and a Rotton Stadium they had become—in fact, if not in name.

Sir Jack Hayward saved the club and rebuilt the stadium—a local man restoring the heart of the community with his generosity—and the council saved the house, restoring it to its former glory and adding an extension to house the city's archives. Perhaps Sir Jack's greatest legacy, when he sold on the club for just £10, was to insist that the stadium would retain its name, and the naming rights would not be sold off for any number of pieces of silver, so that Molineux would always be a name linked with the city of Wolverhampton.

In 2020, Molineux will be celebrating its 300th anniversary. After St Peter's Church, Giffard House, and Queen Square, it is the longest existing institution in Wolverhampton, more famous than all of them, and one with an assured future going into its fourth century.

# 1

# Molineux House

At some time around the year 1720, a building contractor brought his horse and cart, loaded with tools, to High Green in the centre of Wolverhampton—what is now Queen Square. At the upper end, where the 'town hall' then stood at the end of Dudley Street, alongside an open area called the Corn Market, he recruited some of the men who traditionally gathered there, looking for employment to work on a new contract he had been awarded. When he had chosen his men, they walked down High Green to where it split at the lower end with Cock Street to the left and Tup Street to the right.

They went to the right along Tup Street, lined with inns and dwellings. To their right, an open area gave a view across Jennings' gardens to the magnificent St Peter's Church, which dominated the town. They passed Church Alley and Horse Fair, which led by the Pound to The Deanery, the most magnificent house in Wolverhampton. Shortly afterwards, they passed Giffard House on their left and then Wadham's Hill, before almost immediately turning left between a gap in the buildings to an area behind them on Tup Street.

They found themselves in an open area, with land falling away down the hill to marshy flat ground. They had a magnificent view across fields, away to a ridge north of Wolverhampton, beyond the Smestow Brook where the smoke from the houses in the village of Tettenhall curled upwards. To their left, they could see the blue-grey curves of the Wrekin and the Clee Hills, and to their right, they could see Chillington House out in the Staffordshire countryside near the village of Brewood.

A local iron-master named John Rotton had chosen this idyllic spot to build his new house. An iron-master was a man who made and bought and sold the small iron products for which Wolverhampton and the Black Country was becoming famous— locks, hinges, tools, buckles, and all manner of small items. He also bought quantities of pig iron from local smelters and sold it on, often after converting the ingots to wrought iron. A supplier to the many small businesses across the region that were using these iron products, Rotton had become wealthy enough to afford a grand new house for himself and his wife, Jane.

His chosen contractor began work on a fine three-storey house angled to face St Peter's Church to the front, with well laid-out gardens on the terrace behind and 8 acres of land falling away down the hill, bordered by Dunster Lane to the East and

Wadham's Hill, to the west. By all accounts, Rotton was very free with his money, and when he died in 1743, he owed one John Molineux the not inconsiderable sum of £700. His widow and his partner, Richard Wilkes, settled the debt by handing over the house on Wadham's Hill, the transaction being completed in September 1744, a deal largely brokered by Molineux's youngest son, Benjamin.

John Molineux was also an iron-master, supplying the trade's raw materials and then stocking and selling the finished products. He was the son of Richard and Hannah Molineux, born in 1675, possibly in Willenhall. He went into partnership with his elder brother, Daniel, as iron and brass merchants in Dublin, importing their wares from the Black Country, which was beginning to be referred to thus, at about this time. At some period in the 1690s, the brothers became associated with one William Wood who was married to their half sister, Margaret, and whose main residence was The Deanery, the largest house in Wolverhampton, sited to the rear of St Peter's Church, where the Staffordshire Technical College was later built. Wood had invented a machine for mass producing copper coins, and in an early, more basic example of 'printing money', he caused serious inflation in Ireland by overproducing coinage. Whatever his part in his brother-in-law's actions, John Molineux decided to flee the displeasure of the Irish and returned to Wolverhampton and set up as an iron-master in the Horseley Fields area. Daniel remained in Dublin, operating the warehouse there.

In those days, Horseley Fields (Upper and Lower) actually were fields, as the town was much smaller, with the population only reaching around 7,500 in 1750. It was primarily a market town, providing livestock markets for the surrounding countryside, but beginning to exploit plentiful local supplies of coal and iron ore as countless small metal-bashing businesses were set up. He established workshops along the Willenhall Road, the start of which was known as Lower Berry Street, and became a rich and powerful man. In 1702, John married Mary Birch in Willenhall and they were to have five sons and three daughters.

After inspecting his new house, Molineux decided to make it his own residence, though he owned other properties in the town. He had the frontage remodelled in the typical Georgian style of the day, three rows of windows, four at ground level, with a central door, and five at the two upper levels, the third-storey windows being smaller than the others. He also built an extension to the rear, virtually doubling its size. There was a slight difference in the floor levels, front and back, which still exists to this day. Three of his sons had moved to create businesses elsewhere, but his oldest, Thomas, stayed and ran the family's iron business and built himself a home in Dudley Street. When John Molineux died in 1754, Thomas inherited much of the business, but his younger brother, Benjamin, inherited Molineux House, where he lived with his wife, Elizabeth, and had three children.

Benjamin Molineux became something of an entrepreneur, using the family's wealth to finance new businesses such as the new Staffordshire & Worcestershire Canal, in which Elizabeth invested some of her own money. The canal opened in 1772, and via the Birmingham Canal Navigations, which linked to the centre of the town, enabled Wolverhampton's products to be exported easily to the east and west coasts, many of them finding their way to the warehouse in Dublin, which Benjamin had taken over from his uncle. He traded Black Country products with the West Indies and set up a business importing Jamaican rum in return, selling it through a warehouse on North Street, as Tup Street had now become.

This connection led to him being given a three-year-old child, born in Sierra Leone, whom he brought to England and named George John Scipio Africanus. He was baptised in St Peter's Church and educated. He was trained as a hairdresser and then served an apprenticeship in a brass foundry. He left Wolverhampton when he was aged twenty-one and became a successful businessman in Nottingham.

Molineux House, the hub of a business empire, was expanded, with new wings being added over a period of two decades. First was the west wing, like a smaller version of the central, original portion, then the east wing was added, containing all the reception rooms, including a dining room with elaborate rococo plasterwork. Formal gardens were laid out on the plateau behind, and an orchard was planted. Where the ground levelled out near a lane at the bottom of the hill, an ornamental lake was created. For a time, there was a small menagerie of wild animals, and it would be excellent to think that some of them might have been wolves.

Benjamin Molineux died in 1772 and his only son, George, inherited the house and businesses, which he expanded. In 1789, he invested in the town's first newspaper, *The Wolverhampton Chronicle and Staffordshire Advertiser*. As the head of one of the most important families in the town, he became a town commissioner, a forerunner of a councillor, and became high sheriff of Staffordshire and a magistrate.

In 1820, the accession of King George IV was proclaimed publically across the town, a procession of civic leaders, celebrities, and soldiers followed a military band through the streets, with the proclamation being read out before the assembled crowds in four locations, the last being in front of Molineux House, highlighting its importance in the town.

George died that year, having had seven sons and three daughters, and it was one of the younger sons, Charles Henry Molineux, who took possession of the house, buying it from the executors. Charles Henry was a lawyer, but he went into the banking business with Alexander Hordern, establishing the Dudley & West Bromwich Bank with its head office in Dudley Street; Charles Henry was general manager. Unmarried, he lived at Molineux House with his brother, John Edmondson Molineux, and his sister, Sophia, both also unmarried. There were five live-in domestic servants to cater for their needs.

When Charles Henry died in 1848, he left the house to his brother, John Edmondson, who only survived him by three years. He in turn left the house to his nephew, Charles Edward, who was also a lawyer, practicing in Mold, North Wales. Charles Edward moved back to Wolverhampton to live in the house with his wife, Jane, and daughter, Mary, and he also took over the banking business. Sophia died in 1849, leaving Charles Henry as the last Molineux to live in the house.

The expansion of Wolverhampton through the nineteenth century was encroaching on the house from all sides. New terraced housing pressed in at it, immediately to the front, in a development called Molineux Fold. A road down the eastern side of the property came to be called Molineux Street, with terraced houses lining the other side, and the streets built off it. Along the northern side of the property, down the hill, the lane that had marked the boundary was developed into Waterloo Road with much finer dwellings for some of the richer people of the town.

Beyond Waterloo Road, the new suburb of 'Newhampton' was being built. In 1825, a new horse racing course had been constructed at the foot of the hill. Wet ground to the east of Tettenhall Road behind the houses of Waterloo Road was drained, and the

Broadmeadow Racecourse was created. A large grandstand was built in 1827, and over the next ten years, a mile or so of further stands were erected. This was all within the foreground of the view from Molineux House, and though the racecourse might not have been un-panoramic, the streets of terraced houses built to the eastern side of the racecourse on the new roads through the area of Whitmore Reans most certainly were, with smoky coal fires fogging the former fine views out into the Shropshire and Staffordshire countryside.

In 1856, Charles Edward put the house up for sale, including coach house, stables, greenhouse, and conservatory, and he moved his small family out to Kilsall Hall near the village of Cosford. In August 1856, there was a huge sale of household items from Molineux House, but for a further four years, it stood empty, as no one who could afford such a grand house wanted to live in the centre of such urban squalor. Other uses for the house were examined, the Municipal Grammar School even considering it, before deciding to move to Compton Road away from the town centre. For a short while, it was used as a private school, but that was not a success.

It was the 8 acres of ornamental gardens developed at the rear of Molineux House that were to provide the solution for its future. The gardens had been developed into a stunning asset for the town, with an ornamental lake where the ground levelled out near the foot of the hill, and a full time gardener was kept on even after the house was empty to maintain them. This was at a time when a People's Park Movement was advocating the provision of public parks in the industrial towns and cities where residents could promenade on Sundays and enjoy the beneficial aspects of a park, which would also provide an open area where exhibitions and performances could be staged.

A man named Brewster, the owner of the Prince of Wales Music Hall in Bilston Street known locally as The Bucket of Blood, hired the grounds of Molineux House to stage public performances; after 130 years as a private residence, the site had a new use as a place of public entertainment.

Molineux House in the early nineteenth century, a drawing by John Fullwood.

Molineux House and gardens before the clock tower was built on the roof.

**MOLINEUX PLEASURE GROUNDS, WOLVERHAMPTON,**

O. E. McGREGOR. Proprietor

*Above:* The Deanery, the finest house in Wolverhampton, owned by the brother-in-law of John Molineux, William Wood, who had married Margaret Molineux. This house lay behind St Peter's Church.

*Left:* A poster advertising Oliver MacGregor's house and pleasure gardens.

# 2
# Pleasure Gardens

The first event staged by Brewster was Jullien's musical fete on 2 July 1856, which featured open air musical hall acts, singers, and performers. Though many of the people who paid to attend might have been in awe of the beautiful gardens, the whole tone of the event was clearly aimed much lower. One of the 'attractions' was throwing beer bottles into the ornamental lake and being able to bet how long it took for them to sink. The event was clearly a success, because the following year, Brewster repeated it, and this time he added an ascent by hydrogen balloon by the balloonist named John Gray, who ascended in his 'Chinese' balloon, which probably referred to its decoration rather than its manufacture.

Other entrepreneurs took advantage of the site and further fetes were organised, some of a more refined nature, with higher-class artistes and top military bands, and the day's entertainment culminating in firework displays, which included a model warship firing broadsides on the lake and the words 'Thanks to C. E. Molineux Esq.' spelt out in fireworks. Balloon ascents continued to be a feature of the events, but the one at 6.30 p.m. on 13 July 1858 ended in tragedy. A cannon was fired to signal its lift-off, which startled a horse pulling the trap of Joseph Ross, a Bilston butcher, along Waterloo Road. The horse fell over, and as a passer-by was going to the aid of Mr Ross, he was kicked in the head and had to be taken to hospital.

On 13 and 14 September 1858, the celebrated balloonist Henry Coxwell ascended each evening in his balloon, *Queen*, from which a live animal was thrown out to descend by parachute. Such entertainments were the only real use for gas balloons at the time. Two years later, Henry Coxwell was engaged by the scientist James Glaisher to undertake ascents from Wolverhampton Gas Works for scientific purposes, taking measurements in the upper atmosphere. On 5 September 1862, they were to reach a height estimated to be higher than Mount Everest, a World Altitude Record. The 1858 entertainment, as well as the balloon ascent, included a concert, dancing, fireworks, and Chinese lanterns, for the price of just a shilling. A requirement for '1,000 boys for the Chinese Exhibition' was advertised just two weeks before, without any indication of what was involved.

These events drew thousands of paying customers and encouraged the first sporting event to be staged at the Molineux grounds. In 1860, there was a staged repeat of a boxing match between Tom Sayers, 'The Brighton Boy', and the American John C. Heenan, which had been held earlier in the year at Farnborough. There was local interest in Sayers as he had defeated William Perry, 'The Tipton Slasher', a Black Country hero, back in 1851. Hundreds of people turned up to watch, though it was little more than an exhibition match. There was pre-fight entertainment, which included the first public airing of the ballad 'She was only a rat catcher's daughter', which apparently brought many spectators to tears.

The success of such events alerted Charles Molineux to the possibility of selling his house not as a private residence but as a site for 'a public institution ... also well adapted for a first class hotel, the want of one being much felt in Wolverhampton', and it was advertised for sale as such in April 1859. It was to be a year before anyone took the gamble of buying the house and gardens as a commercial proposition, and that man was Oliver Edgar McGregor.

McGregor was a Scotsman who had come to Wolverhampton and became rich running a business importing tobacco from America. He also owned a restaurant on High Green and a large house, with 22 acres of land, in Finchfield. He had become a man of influence in the town and had the support of the long-serving MP Charles Villiers and Mayor Thomas Bantock. He invested a huge sum of money in his new venture, something around £7,000, enlarging the lake so rowing boats could be hired, planting the gardens with shrubs, and advertising the beauty of the garden for people to come and enjoy, for the entrance fee of a shilling, even outside the regular summer fetes that he continued to run.

New attractions were added to the gardens, including high-wire acts and a version of the Highland Games. He introduced team sports for the first time, including cricket, lacrosse, and croquet, and then introduced the new sport of cycle racing, with a track around the ornamental lake. The natural metal-bashing skills found throughout the town had naturally led to many local companies turning their hands to making bicycles, a new craze that was sweeping the land. By the end of the 1860s, there were nearly thirty bicycle makers in the town.

MacGregor clearly had a struggle to make ends meet to begin with, as he was forced to reduce the entrance fee from a shilling to 6d, and then, on quiet days, it was reduced again to 2d. A big boost came in 1868 when a group of eminent men approached him to hire Molineux House and Gardens for the South Staffordshire Industrial and Fine Arts Exhibition to showcase local industrial products and artists. A large committee was formed to organise and to promote the Exhibition, which opened on 10 May 1869.

The house was clearly not big enough to house all the exhibits and so a cast-iron building, 150 feet long and 60 feet wide, with corrugated-iron cladding was designed and erected on the flat area to the eastern end of the house. This cost £2,376, a considerable sum for the 200 backers who had come forward. The hall contained the work of 130 local manufacturers, including working models of steam engines and a lighthouse. There was a stage for a bandstand at one end. A balcony ran around the edges where hundreds of works of art were displayed, with more inside the house, which was used as the main entrance. In fact, there were 688 paintings loaned from collections across Great Britain. There were tea rooms, and even the old stables were used for a display of Royal Costumes. A further 3 acres of the gardens were used for more displays and the gardens were remodelled for the event.

Once more the entrance fee was set too high at a shilling per person, and only after it was halved did visitor numbers become satisfactory. In addition, combined rail tickets/ entry tickets brought people from all over England. The exhibition was open for 142 days, and in that time, there were 222,000 visitors, making it a financial success. Oliver MacGregor had an assured rent for the use of his property, but perhaps his greatest benefit was the publicity it created for the Molineux.

MacGregor had come to realise that he needed more than just beautiful gardens to attract paying visitors, and he saw sporting contests as the solution. For the first time, the people of Wolverhampton could go to an evening match at the Molineux, though it would normally be cricket, by the likes of the Wolverhampton and Bridgnorth Tradesmen's Clubs or Wolverhampton *versus* Wolverhampton Rovers Cricket Clubs. He promoted lacrosse, cricket, and football matches, and particularly the new sport of cycle racing. He had an elliptical track built around an enlarged lake at the flat northern end of the garden, allowing provision for spectators up the hill. Molineux was now promoted as Pleasure Gardens and Cycle Track, and through the 1870s, large crowds came to see cycle races between famous riders of the day, over distances of 1–50 miles; local manufacturers vied with one another following the dictum that Competition Sells, and they used the track to test new designs. To begin with, what we would call penny-farthing bicycles held sway, but increasingly 'safety' bicycles, the kind we are familiar with today, were developed to be competitive.

In fact, Molineux now came to be seen as the home of cycle racing in Great Britain and crowds increased. On Boxing Day 1875, a crowd of 18,000 people watched four of the greatest riders of the day—Fred Cooper, James Moore, John Keen, and David Stanton—compete in a series of races. The following year, the Frenchman Camille Thuillet established a World Endurance Record by riding a bicycle for six days with very few permitted stops, with 10,000 people paying to watch. In 1877, the Wolverhampton Cycle Club was formed, with Molineux as its base. By 1886, such was the prestige of the venue, the International Bicycle World Championships were held there.

The interior of the temporary pavilion built for the South Staffordshire Fine Arts and Industries Exhibition.

The mayor declares the Fine Arts and Industries exhibition open.

The temporary cast iron-framed exhibition building built to the right of Molineux House, a picture taken from the far side of the ornamental lake.

Deanery Row, an example of the low-quality housing to be found around Wolverhampton, encroaching close to the front of Molineux House.

A hydrogen balloon ascent in front of a large crowd at the Molineux in 1888. The grandstand was for the cycle racing on the track around the lake. Col. Thorneycroft of Tettenhall was a passenger in the balloon, which failed to rise much above the roof tops as it flew slowly across the Black Country.

Hudson's Soap giving tethered balloon ascents to people with sufficient vouchers, taking off from the football pitch in May 1901.

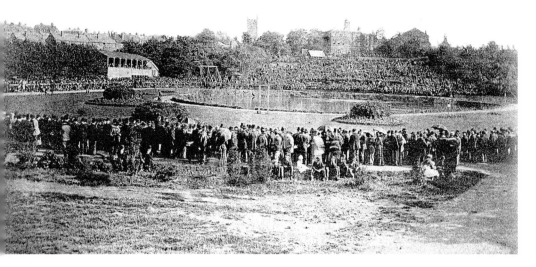

A huge crowd gathered to watch cycle racing, and an evening balloon ascent in 1888.

Broadmeadow racecourse looking towards the town centre. Molineux House out of view to the left.

A view of the town centre from Five Ways on the Stafford Road in the late nineteenth century.

Molineux Hotel when it had a third bowling green at the front, as well as the two at the rear.

# 3
# Molineux Hotel

With cycle racing established in the gardens, MacGregor now sought to exploit the house itself, turning it into a hotel. His drinks licence was granted on 30 August 1871, and over the next fifteen years, the house was slowly adapted to its new role, with a bar, dining room, billiard room, and bedrooms. Creating something of a lasting landmark for the town, MacGregor paid for the clock tower to be erected on the roof of the hotel in 1876. Partly to attract customers into the bar, and also to utilise the flat area created for the exhibition, he laid out the first of three bowling greens around the hotel, and the Molineux Bowling Club was established, becoming one of the most prestigious in the town.

Ever eager to grasp a new fad, MacGregor—possibly at the suggestion of a new partner named Wiley who appeared on the scene in the mid-1870s—dug up the bowling green at the rear of the house and created a concrete ellipse, 200 feet long and 90 feet wide, to be used as an ice skating rink in the winter and a rolling skating rink in the warmer seasons. This skating venture was short lived—the winter season was short and roller skates were too expensive for the average family—and the bowling green was eventually restored.

The hotel was doing well as the decade ended, but with West Park opening half a mile away in 1881, on the former Broadmeadow Racecourse, no one was willing to pay to wander around Molineux's gardens. He attempted to replicate the success of the Industrial and Arts Exhibition with a similar but smaller event held in 1878, but it had nowhere near the impact of that held in 1869.

In 1884, MacGregor was approaching retirement age and had sunk the equivalent of £1 million in improvements and additions to Molineux, but now perhaps the endless endeavour was taking its toll and he placed Molineux on the market. It was bought by a local bacon butcher named Edwin Steer, and MacGregor retired to his property in Finchfield.

Steer did not have much chance to make his mark on the property as he died two years later; a local builder named J. E. Gittoes then obtained ownership for a very short while before putting it on the market again. On 6 June 1887, Molineux House and grounds were put up for sale by public auction and were sold to Joseph Devy, publican of the Bricklayer's Arms in Walsall Street, for the sum of £5,850. It might be that Devy bought the property on behalf of the Northampton Brewery, because they owned it by 1889. The hotel was clearly the prize for the brewery, who had little use for the gardens, and sought a new owner for them, and a local football club seemed prime candidates—though it was not the team that is now associated with the ground, but the Stafford Roaders.

*Left:* Bowlers enjoying afternoon games on the two greens at the rear of the hotel.

*Below:* The terrace of the hotel and the two bowling greens, with the houses of Molineux Street in the background.

THE DRAW WILL BE STRICTLY ADHERED TO.

| MOLINEUX. | | ST. GILES', WILLENHALL. | |
|---|---|---|---|
| 1—J. COLLINS | 21 | 1—P. MILLINGTON | 20 |
| 2—A. TONKS | 16 | 2—O. FARRINGTON | 21 |
| 3—F. TOMLINSON | 21 | 3—H. TONKINSON | 8 |
| 4—L. SQUIRE (Captain) | 21 | 4—W. JOHNSON | 16 |
| 5—E. P. BQSI | 21 | 5—A. FARRINGTON | 12 |
| 6—W. TORRINGTON | 21 | 6—T. HADDON | 9 |
| 7—W. LOWE | 21 | 7—J. GLOTHAM | 8 |
| 8—H. PRESTON | 18 | 8—J. WAKELAM | 21 |
| 9—W. E. HARRISON | 21 | 9—E. EDGE | 10 |
| 10—H. COOK | 21 | 10—J. AMOS | 12 |
| 11—J. GOUGH | 21 | 11—F. SANDERS, Junr. | 8 |
| 12—*H. Norris* | 17 | 12—T. PARKER | 21 |
| 13—O. BARTLAM | 21 | 13—J. GROCOTT | 15 |
| 14—W. STEVENSON | 21 | 14—F. SANDERS, Senr. (Captain) | 12 |
| 15—E. WALTERS | 21 | 15—A. HICKS | 6 |
| 16—H. TOMLINSON | 20 | 16—F. EVANS | 20 |
| Reserves: E. Price, H. Norris. | 323 | Reserves: A. Broome, E. Gibbons. | 220 |

N.B.—ONLY 10 MINUTES' GRACE WILL BE ALLOWED, AFTER WHICH A RESERVE MAN WILL BE CALLED UPON.

*Molineux won by 103*

A scorecard showing a convincing victory for Molineux Bowling Club *versus* St Giles, Willenhall.

Molineux Fold with the four terraced cottages to the right, the end of the billiard hall to the left.

The hotel dining room taken from a Butler's brochure printed in 1928.

The hall, a room that was part of the original house built in 1720 and which remains the entrance to the building to this day.

*Right:* The oak room adjacent to the hallway has fine panelling and also dates from the original house. The panelling had been removed and placed into store, luckily, before the fire that nearly destroyed the house and has since been restored.

*Below:* The interior of the billiard hall built alongside Molineux Alley.

"MOLINEUX" BILLIARD HALL, WOLVERHAMPTON.

# 4

# Molineux Stadium

In the 1860s, football spread like wildfire across Great Britain, and many clubs sprang up in Wolverhampton, some attached to companies like Great Western Railway's Stafford Road Works, others to suburbs like Whitmore Reans and Wednesfield. On the other side of the town from Molineux, St Luke's Church had a school alongside from 1861. In 1877, two pupil teachers, John Baynton and John Brodie, who had been given a ball by the twenty-one-year-old headmaster, Harry Barcroft, formed a football team at the suggestion of Feargus Hill, father of one of the pupils. Blakenhall St Luke's FC, as it was known initially, met in the King's Arms public house on the Dudley Road and used the Old Windmill Field as its first pitch. The first competitive match was against the Stafford Roaders Second XI, and they lost 0:8.

The club did well, and within two years, a better ground was needed, and so St Luke's moved to John Harper Field in Lower Villiers Street, opposite Stroud's Niphon Works, a factory building that is still there. They stayed there until the summer of 1881, when they amalgamated with a cricket club called Blakenhall Wanderers who used a ground by the Fighting Cocks. The cricket club insisted that the football club change its name, so they became Wolverhampton Wanderers. They also changed their strip from blue to red and white stripes, though by the end of a season of shirt washing, they were more like pink and white stripes.

Over the next eight years, the Wanderers became a powerful club, taking on and beating clubs from other towns like Stoke, and even playing the top club in the country, Preston, the team that would become The Invincibles in the first Football League season. Nevertheless, the Wanderers were not the top team in Wolverhampton—that honour went to the GWR Stafford Road Engine Works team, The Roaders, founded in 1876, and which reached the semi-final of the FA Cup in 1881, being defeated by the Old Etonians. The Roaders played on a pitch in Fox's Lane, in their red and black kit, but such was their strength—with several English internationals in their ranks—that they often played important matches at the Molineux.

In the 1886–7 season, they listed 'The Molineux Bicycle Grounds' as their pitch and their first and second elevens played twenty matches there. Through the 1880s, the Roaders and the Wanderers vied with one another to become the best team in Wolverhampton, but whenever they met, the Wanderers generally won, including in the FA Cup, and when winning their first piece of silverware, The Wrekin Cup.

Wolverhampton Wanderers took part in the FA Cup for the first time in 1883, beating Long Eaton Rangers in their first tie 4:1, but losing to Wednesbury Old Athletic in the next round. The following year, a Walsall Cup Tie against Walsall Swifts was played at Molineux, and around 4,000 spectators attended—about twice their usual crowd.

They were assured of their pre-eminence in the town when they became one of the twelve founder members of the Football League in 1888. The Wanderers' very first league match was at the Dudley Road ground against Aston Villa, which ended 1:1. In that first season, unbeaten Preston were champions, Villa came second, and the Wanderers third, and the FA Cup final took place at Kennington Oval between Wolves and Preston, the latter doing the double with a 3:0 victory.

The club was now one of the pre-eminent teams in the country, with many English internationals in its ranks, and clearly the Dudley Road ground was in need of replacement. The Stafford Roaders had faded in importance and could not sustain their hold on Molineux, and the Wolves decided to move across town. Northampton Brewery were happy to charge a rent of just £50 per year. During the summer of 1889, workmen tore up the gardens, filled in the lake, cut down trees, and constructed cinder-covered embankments for the crowd, including a covered area for 4,000 spectators. Offices and changing rooms were built next to Molineux Street, in the corner, and the grandstand halfway along the Molineux Street side was inherited from the cycle racing days. A new stand holding just 300 spectators was erected on the Waterloo Road side of the ground. As well as the new ground, the team acquired a new appearance when the pink and white strip was ditched and the old gold and black, which was said to reflect the town's motto *Out of darkness cometh light*, was adopted,

The first match at the new ground was to be a friendly *versus* Aston Villa on 2 September 1889, and although the reconstruction work was not finished, the new pitch was in perfect condition and a great improvement on the bumpy old Dudley Road ground. Wolves won 1:0, and the honour of scoring the first goal at the new stadium fell to David Wykes, who also scored the first league goal a week later in a 2:0 victory over Notts County. After the Villa friendly, a banquet was held in the Molineux Hotel for all concerned, and an association between Wolverhampton's football club and the name Molineux was cemented, lasting to this day.

With new tenants in the grounds, Northampton Brewery decided to appoint a new landlord to the hotel. A man named Dade was in place when they acquired the property, but they now appointed a twenty-nine-year-old named Walter George from Cane in Wiltshire. He and his family moved into the living quarters upstairs, and new staff were employed, including a handyman who oversaw the removal of the skating ring and the restoration of the bowling green. The hotel became a sporting hub. One of the last additions made by Oliver MacGregor was the erection of a new building along Molineux Alley to the west side and the installation of twelve billiard tables. Whether playing bowls or billiards, or using the assembly room and ballroom for weddings, dances, or meetings, Molineux Hotel became a gathering place for the town.

Apart from being the registered home of the Wolves, and the location of board meetings until club offices were built on Waterloo Road in the 1920s, the hotel also hosted regional meetings of the Football League and the Football Association. A number of international matches were to be played there, starting in season 1890–91 when England drubbed Ireland 6:1 in front of 15,000 spectators.

The 1901 Ordnance Survey Map of the town shows small covered embankments along the Waterloo Road side of the ground, incorporating the 300-seat stand, and along the north side of the ground up to the triangular changing rooms/directors' stand/office on the edge of Molineux Street. Apart from the old cycle racing stand, the whole of the Molineux Street side and the huge embankment at the 'Hotel end' were open shale-covered banks.

In 1902, electric trams arrived in Waterloo Road. The corporation's new surface-contact electric tram tracks were first laid from the Depot in Cleveland Road, via High Level Station to West Park where a huge Arts and Industry Exhibition took place that summer. The first small extension to the system was a short spur from the top of Newhampton Road down Waterloo Road to the stadium entrance so fans arriving for a match could do so by tram. This spur was later extended to become the start of the route to Bushbury.

A new licensee took over the running of the hotel shortly after Wolves moved to the new ground, a man of major importance in the history of the club, Jack Addenbrooke. He had attended St Luke's School and was one of the founders of the football club; in fact, he was made secretary at the tender age of ten. He was to go to Saltley College, Birmingham, and trained as a teacher, returning to teach at Bushbury School, but also turning out regularly for the reserves from 1883. In August 1885, he was appointed as the first paid secretary/manager of the football club, and he oversaw the move to the Molineux.

He remained secretary/manager for a record twenty-seven years until 1922, and apart from organising the move to the new stadium and the club's entry into the Football League, he led the team to five FA Cup finals, winning two (in 1893 and 1908) and losing the others (in 1889, 1896, and 1921). As well as running the football club and the hotel, he also owned a tobacconist shop in the town.

Northampton Brewery sold Molineux Hotel to Wolverhampton's Butler's Brewery in October 1897, having found the distance it had to make deliveries a drain on its profits. Jack Addenbrooke had enough on his plate running the football club and developing the stadium, and he gave up managing the hotel in November 1900. Butler's appointed one George Chamberlain to replace him, but over the next dozen years, there were a whole series of new landlords, clearly the job running such a large establishment was a tough one. In February 1906, it was decided to split the 'downstairs' and 'upstairs' sides of the business; William Wyke was appointed the hotel licensee and Joseph Guy took the alcohol licence.

Butler's instituted a number of changes around the property. All but four of the terraced houses that lined the entrance from North Street were demolished with the 'courts' that lay behind them. Such 'courts' were a feature of the cheap lower-class housing in the town. Some of the resulting land was given to the council, and some was eventually used to create a car park, as motoring became more common among the hotel's clientele.

In the 1904–5 season, Wolves finished bottom of Division One and were relegated for the first time. They spent a total of twenty-nine years out of the top flight, though some of those were during the First World War when league football was suspended. Nevertheless, they achieved a monumental victory in the FA Cup in 1908, beating Newcastle United, the outstanding team of the day, 3:1 in the final at Crystal Palace, watched by an astonishing 74,967 spectators. The victory created huge excitement in the town, and may have led to some ground improvements being made in 1910, when the stands on the Waterloo Road and north sides were enlarged and given new roofs at second-storey height. The north stand had a pronounced dog-leg, and its curved Dutch barn-type roof led to it being nicknamed The Cowshed.

The hotel remained one of the best in town and attracted a lot of actors and music hall artistes from the Empire Theatre, which lay at the bottom of Queen Square near the start of North Street. Wyke and Guy ran the hotel between them for eight years, and then in the summer of 1914, Albert Paulton was appointed to run the whole operation, and the Paulton family became one of those most associated with the Molineux.

Albert Paulton ran a printing business in Berry Street with his brothers, and printed the Wolves' club programmes and other literature. He had shares in the club and was a director for a time; he was also a town alderman. His son, George Henry, who was generally known as Harry, married a Wednesfield girl named Mary Ellen Shotton just before the start of the First World War. The couple moved into Molineux Hotel before Harry went off to war, and Mary Ellen gave birth to a daughter on Christmas Eve 1915. Harry was to return from the war and took over the hotel from his father in December 1919, keeping the licence for another decade.

Albert Paulton was the instigator of the creation of the Molineux Bowling Club based on the hotel, and he was the club's first president, holding the role until 1926. The club was one of the most famous in the Midlands, not least because of the size of its green, which was the largest in the country. Paulton was also president of the Staffordshire County Bowling Association from 1917, and the hotel was used as its headquarters.

Apart from sports clubs, many other organisations held meetings at the hotel, including the T&GW Union, the Football Association, the Referee's Association, the Royal Ancient Order of the Buffaloes, and even the Boy Scouts and Girl Guides.

When the First World War began, the authorities thought at first football would be good for morale, and the 1914–5 season took place, with Wolves ending up in fourth place in the Second Division. With losses mounting on the Western Front and it becoming clear that the war would not end soon, football was then suspended. Molineux was made available for local teams playing charity matches. The football teams of major local companies like Guy Motors and the Sunbeam Motor Car Co., as well as Army teams, all played matches at the Molineux.

 With the war over, a short regional Victory League was organised, for the abbreviated 1918–9 season, which allowed clubs to reorganise themselves. Wolves were to play six matches, winning two and drawing three. They were still wearing their gold and black stripes, but there is some evidence to suggest that it was the more vibrant gold of later years.

The Football League restarted the following season with Wolves still in the Second Division. There was a huge appetite for football and the crowds flooded back, but after an unbeaten first six games, Wolves fell away and were to finish the season in nineteenth place. Jack Addenbrooke was still the combined secretary/manager and he took the team to another cup final the following year, but there was to be no upset against their First Division opposition, Tottenham Hotspur, this time, as they were beaten 1:0 at Stamford Bridge

Addenbrooke led them for another disappointing season the following year, but in 1922–3, he was replaced by George Robey, only for the team to finish bottom and be relegated to the Third Division (North). They spent only one year in the depths, being promoted as champions in 1924.

Despite the team being in the lower divisions, the directors set about the total redevelopment of the ground between the wars. This began in a small way in 1921 with the erection of a directors' area next to the small triangular building at the corner of the Molineux Street stand and the North End. A local architect, Marcus Browne, had designed the Waterloo Road stand, built in 1909, and when his advice was sought, he was instrumental in bringing in Archibald Leitch, a specialist in sports stadium design. In consultations between Leitch, Browne, and the board, the state-of-the-art new Waterloo Road stand emerged. The stand was two-tiered, with a wooden upper seated area and a lower standing enclosure, covered by a new roof on purpose-built structural steelwork. The changing rooms and club offices were to be moved into this new stand, which had a pronounced dog-leg shape.

A contract was issued in 1924 to build a steel structure over the open Molineux Street stand to take the old Waterloo Stand roof. Unfortunately, this partial cover for the Molineux Street spectators did not last long, as in January 1925, a gale blew the roof over and into Molineux Street, together with much of the boundary wall on which it was built. The new Waterloo Road stand was largely finished for the opening of the 1925–6 Season on 29 August.

Molineux Hotel was also being redeveloped about this time; in 1926, new bedrooms were added. It was handy for owners and trainers from Dunstall Park Racecourse to stay, as well as American executives visiting to oversee the construction of the giant Goodyear Factory not far away.

The two bowling greens at the rear of the hotel continued to be well patronised and afforded a fine view down the terracing of the 'Hotel End' to the football pitch. Harry Paulton kept the licence of the hotel until 1928. He was a keen bowler himself, and also a member of the Staffordshire Casuals Cricket Club. When he left the Molineux to manage the Market Tavern in Cheapside, there followed a whole series of custodians of the Molineux Hotel up to 1933, when Harry Armitage took over and was to remain in charge through the Second World War.

The football club finally climbed back out of the Second Division in 1932 as champions, with Major Frank Buckley becoming manager in 1927; he ruled with an iron hand. In May, plans for the redevelopment of the North End and the Molineux Street sides of the ground, designed by Archie Leitch, were approved by the council. The old structures were demolished, including the old offices/changing room area in the corner, and new stands erected. The construction took little more than eight weeks, with steelwork from Rubery Owen.

The North Bank, as it was now called, straightened out that end of the ground with a conventional stand, but it was the Molineux Street stand that became the iconic feature of the new Molineux. Leitch designed a seven-gable roof to fill the long triangle between the edge of the pitch and the edge of Molineux Street itself. Each bay from the lower end was longer than the next, with seats for 3,450 spectators on the upper tier and a standing area at the front.

Redevelopment of the ground was completed in 1936 when a roof and other facilities were erected over the upper end of the vast South Bank terrace. Complaints from fans that they could now no longer see the clock on the top of Molineux Hotel—to learn how much time was left in the match that they were watching—was solved by the club after a board meeting in July 1936; a new clock was ordered for installation in the centre gable of the Molineux Street Stand and the instantly recognisable panorama of the ground from the main Waterloo Road Stand was complete, remaining thus for the next sixty years.

The ground redevelopment was complete and Molineux had become one of the best stadiums in the country, just as Wolves were becoming one of the best teams in the country. After a shaky start in the top flight, the team came fifth in the league in 1936–7, and then with Stan Cullis as centre half and captain, they came second two years in a row. The team went to the cup final in 1939, where they suffered a shock defeat to Portsmouth. The new stadium was able to host a record 61,315 spectators for the FA Cup fifth round against Liverpool.

Just as Major Buckley's young side had become one of the greatest in the land, gracing a virtually new stadium that was as good as any, the Second World War intervened. The Football League was suspended for the duration, but various regional competitions continued. Many footballers served in the armed forces and often guested for clubs around the country; Wolves were no different. Perhaps the most famous of the players who guested for them during the war were two local brothers, Jack and Arthur Rowley, who had both been born in the town and educated at Dudley Road School. The elder brother, Jack, started on Wolves books but never made the first team, and it was at Manchester United that he made his name, becoming their all-time top scorer with 211 goals in 424 matches over a seventeen-year period. Arthur also started in Wolves reserves but then went to West Brom, Fulham, Leicester, and Shrewsbury, holding the all-time Football League scorer record with 434 goals in 619 matches. Both brothers were to guest for their hometown club several times during the war while home on leave.

During the war, the South Bank was commandeered for the storage of empty shell cases before their delivery to be filled in munitions factories, and the secure area beneath the stand was turned into the local air-raid shelter, available to the staff and guests in the hotel. The roof of the hotel became a site for the perilous job of fire watching. Whenever there was an air raid, and everyone else was down in the shelters, the firewatchers would be on duty at lofty places like the hotel roof and the top of Tettenhall Church across the valley, looking out for the fall of bombs, ready to direct the emergency services to the scene. Thankfully, there were very few air raids on Wolverhampton—just the odd bomber disgorging its load.

The hotel remained open during the war, though its guests were increasingly in uniform. Its ballroom remained open for dances, popular with local servicemen, from the RAF stations at Cosford, Wolverhampton, and Perton and the Dutch soldiers stationed at Wrottesley Park. The hotel's fine rooms remained a popular choice for wedding receptions.

On 8 May 1945, VE Day was proclaimed and there were wild celebrations across the town, not least in the bars of the Molineux Hotel; a few days later, Victory Sunday was celebrated in the stadium, with over 10,000 people attending,

The Football League resumed for the 1946–7 season, and Wolves had a new manager in Ted Vizard, recruited from QPR. Shortly afterwards, his captain, Stan Cullis, retired and became Vizard's assistant. A born leader, Cullis had been appointed the Wolves captain when only twenty years old; he became England's captain aged twenty-two. The war abbreviated his career, as he served in the Army in Italy, and it was no surprise that he became a company sergeant-major.

The Wolves came third and fifth under Vizard, and then Cullis took over as manager. In his first season, the team came sixth in the First Division and won the FA Cup. Cullis was succeeded as captain by another inspirational centre half, Billy Wright, and the two led the Wolves into their most successful decade, making them the best team in the land.

The team were second in 1950, followed by two poor seasons, but then they were third in 1953, and the Holy Grail of the League Championship finally arrived in 1954.

With Johnny Hancocks and Dennis Wilshaw both scoring twenty-five goals and Roy Swinbourne twenty-four, they finally became champions of England. That season saw one other notable first at the Molineux: the first set of floodlights were installed at the start of the campaign, though they were not used for the first league match, first seeing use in April 1956. Nevertheless, floodlit friendlies became a significant feature of the stadium, with some of the great teams from Europe taking part. Spartak Moscow were defeated 4:0 in November 1954, and then a month later came the Hungarian champions, Honved, who fielded many of the Hungarian side that humiliated England 3:6 at Wembley; Wolves won 3:2. Over the next few years, Moscow Dynamo and Real Madrid came and were defeated, and the spectacle of mid-week floodlit matches helped inspire the creation of the European Cup

In 1957, the floodlights were replaced with new ones set on the top of four 146-foot-high pylons, the greatest visual change to the Molineux since the South Bank roof had been erected. Mid-week matches now literally lit up the terraced streets around the ground, and the glow of the pylons could be seen across the town, and the roar of the crowd could be heard and interpreted as far away as Claregate.

There were changes at the hotel as well. The widespread destruction of many of the nation's old buildings, caused by the Luftwaffe, led to significant buildings being protected from developers by listing them in several categories. In July 1949, the Molineux Hotel had been given Grade II listed status as one of the most important buildings in Wolverhampton. It remained an entertainment centre for the town, the Friday and Saturday night dances continued to be popular, and wedding receptions and other gatherings filled the rooms. The crown green bowlers still used the facilities, and the billiard hall next to Molineux Alley remained popular until it fell into a poor state of repair and was demolished in 1958.

This date might be seen as a watershed moment for the hotel. Its popularity as a hotel had declined through the 1950s, its facilities seeming old fashioned, and it had become just a large public house, albeit with enough room for two or three wedding receptions and other events to take place at the same time.

The team, too, was reaching a watershed moment. They won the league again in 1958 and 1959, and then the FA Cup in 1960, just failing to do the double by one point. One more goal in a drawn match would have seen them triumph over Burnley by goal advantage. They had not progressed far in their first two European Cup campaigns, and though they reached the semi-final of the European Cup Winners' Cup in 1961, and came third in the league, that was the summit for Cullis' team. Billy Wright had retired at the end of 1959, and many of the other players needed replacing.

The team fell into the doldrums, Cullis was replaced, and in 1965, they were relegated for the second time into the Second Division, where they spent two seasons. The hotel declined in popularity at the same time, and in 1969, the new inner ring road running near its doorstep cut it off from the town centre, and much of the housing along North Street was demolished, leaving reduced local clientele for the surviving pubs, the Feathers and the Fox, with Molineux Hotel the most isolated. Butler's Brewery had been taken over by Birmingham's Mitchells & Butlers in the early '60s, and that close local connection was lost. There was a lack of investment in the building, and with no local trade and competition from town centre night clubs, the Brewery finally sold the hotel to the football club in 1976, the two parts of the Molineux story were reunited again.

The club had undertaken a revival in the 1970s under the management of Bill McGarry, winning the League Cup in 1974, qualifying for Europe three times by league position, and reaching the final of the UEFA Cup. They applied to demolish the hotel to make way for car parking, but the council refused, and had its listing upgraded to Grade II* status, the following year, just before it closed in 1979 because of poor trading figures.

The club had been buying up properties, particularly on the other side of Molineux Street, for some time, and any plausible expansion of the stadium was restricted by the roads on two sides, and the board was planning ahead. The team had been relegated again in 1976, but came straight back up as champions the following year under the management of Sammy Chung, who had been Bill McGarry's assistant. After two seasons in the doldrums, John Barnwell became manager and things looked up; they came sixth in Division One and won the League Cup once again. At the start of the season, they had paid a British record fee to bring in Andy Gray, and he scored the winner in the final. Things were improving, and ground expansion plans were finally put into gear.

The club had produced a plan to build a 70,000-capacity stadium back in 1958, but that had not progressed beyond a fine model. Now they initiated a stage-by-stage redevelopment, which would lead to an all-new 40,000-seat stadium by 1984; this would begin with a brand-new stand built on top of Molineux Street, partly because the old stand had not passed a recent safety review. They applied for and received permission to knock down the houses on the other side of Molineux Street, and the new 9,348-seat stand, with forty-two executive boxes, was built behind the existing stand, which was then demolished in the close season.

The new stand was opened for the start of the successful 1979–80 season, with the pitch moved over 100 feet so that it no longer lined up with the two ends of the ground. The rest of the redevelopment was not to be. Interest charges on the money borrowed for the new stand rose beyond expectations, and the team did poorly in the next two seasons and were relegated yet again in 1982. It is likely that the poor atmosphere the new ground generated might have something to do with the team's poor form.

The summer of 1982 saw the club struggling with debts of £2.4 million, as well as being faced with a season in the Second Division. It came very close to going out of existence, but at the last minute, a company called Allied Properties (owned by two Saudi Arabian brothers named Bhatti) and former player Derek Dougan (as Chief Executive) stepped in to take over. The club was saved, and despite no investment in the team, the new manager, Graham Hawkins, somehow got them promoted again the following season.

This turned out to be a false dawn, and they were relegated again after one season in the top flight, and then began a plummet through the divisions, shedding managers and players like leaves from a falling tree. In their third relegation in a row, in the 1985–6 season, a second blow struck the club after the Bradford City fire. The old wooden Waterloo Road stand and North Bank were condemned as unsafe and were closed, never to open again. The team had fallen into the Fourth Division for the first time, with a ground that only had two sides. Alongside the decaying stadium, Molineux Hotel lay empty and derelict with broken windows and was sold to Waterloo Properties. The name Molineux had become an embarrassment.

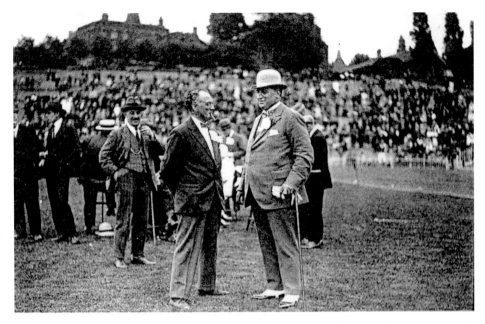

David Webster, Chief Constable of Wolverhampton, (right) standing on the pitch with club directors and other dignitaries.

The souvenir menu from the banquet at the Victoria Hotel, celebrating the 1908 FA Cup win, listing players and officials.

The original Molineux Stadium in 1908, with the Waterloo Road stand in two distinct parts to the left. The houses visible behind are still there. The hotel end in the foreground was just a vast cinder bank.

The view of the stadium from the hotel was excellent, looking across the bowling greens and down a crowded south end terrace. The cinder bank was always a cause of complaint, making spectators' ankles ache. The Molineux Street stand is curved away from the pitch, and the small triangular offices/changing room building lies in the corner.

*Left:* One of the most important men in the history of the Wolves was Jack Addenbrooke, who was club secretary at St Luke's on formation and became secretary/manager from 1885 to 1922. He was also licensee of the hotel for a while.

*Below:* The team that won the FA Cup in 1908 when still in the Second Division. Jack Addenbrooke is on the right, showing the gold and black stripes that they wore for many years.

A walk to the ground from Queen Square might start off down North Street by the town hall, which can just be seen in the haze in the background. The Guy trolley bus is circling the small roundabout, which was at the top of Darlington Street, dating this image to the late 1920s.

A little further down North Street, fans would pass the Queen's Hotel on Cheapside.

Cheapside lay between the retail market and the rear of the Hippodrome, with St Peter's lurking in the mist in the background.

A little further on, these buildings lay on the left-hand side of North Street where the civic hall/telephone exchange now lie.

*Right:* Opposite those buildings was
the open air market, seen here in the
nineteenth century.

*Below:* These buildings lay just before
Molineux Fold, which can be seen in the
background. The ring road now runs
through this area.

The entrance to Molineux Fold and the Hotel, with North Street falling away into the distance towards Five Ways.

Molineux Fold after all but four of the terraced houses and the courts behind them had been demolished by Butler's Brewery, and land had been given to the council.

The start of Molineux Street, which led down the east side of the football ground.

The mean housing that lay along North Street.

The Feathers on North Street, just below Molineux Street, the only building that is still there today, though no longer a pub.

These buildings were probably on North Street, when Molineux House was built.

George Henry Paulton and his wife, Mary Shotten. Harry Poulton, as he was always known, was the second of the family to take on the Molineux Hotel.

The Paulton Brothers on the steps at the rear of the Molineux Hotel. They ran a printing business in Berry Street, and Albert (on the right) became licence of the hotel in 1914 and through the war years.

Albert Paulton on one of the two circus elephants who used to famously overwinter in Wolverhampton, either Salt or Saucy.

Troops of the Staffordshire Regiment receive a mayoral send off between the indoor retail market and St Peter's. The Molineux is a few yards beyond the wholesale market in the background.

*Above:* A wedding party on the rear steps of the Molineux Hotel, which was a popular venue for weddings right up until the 1950s when this one took place.

*Right:* Albert Paulton, licensee of Molineux Hotel from 1914 to 1919.

Two ladies enjoy the sunshine on one of Molineux Hotel's benches in the 1930s. Throughout its existence, the building afforded a fine panorama from here.

Throughout the First World War, the hotel remained a popular venue but the customers now regularly were in uniform.

Though this aerial photo was taken in the 1950s, apart from the floodlight pylons, it represents the redevelopment of the stadium that took place between the wars. The dog-leg Waterloo Road stand was the first built, along with the North Bank, which replaced the old dog-leg 'Cowshed'; Archie Lieth's iconic Molineux Street stand, with its seven-bay roof, was next, followed by the roof over the rear of the South Bank. The hotel, with its bowling greens, lies behind.

The Archie Leith Waterloo Road stand, into which the club offices and changing rooms were moved, with wooden upper seating terrace and a standing enclosure at the front. The TV gantry on the roof was added in the '60s.

Molineux's own 'twin towers', the rear of the Waterloo Road stand, as first built. Later on, there was further building work, infilling this area.

Wolves play Arsenal in the 1930s, with the huge South Bank terrace holding up to 20,000 spectators. Stan Cullis watches his goalkeeper deal with things.

Stan Cullis signs a football surrounded by the Wolves team, which became such a force in the late 1930s.

Stan Cullis leads the team out at Molineux, between the dug-outs at the Waterloo Road stand. This scene was to be repeated for the next sixty years with different captains, often to the tune 'The Happy Wanderer'.

*Left*: Stan Cullis introduces the king to the team at Wembley before the 1939 FA Cup Final against Portsmouth, which ended in a disappointing defeat.

*Below*: Stan Cullis, Billy Wright, and the FA Cup winning team of 1949.

Molineux Hotel in the 1960s after the billiard hall had been demolished, with the gates leading down to the South Bank turnstiles to the left.

A trolley bus climbs Molineux Street, with the Molineux Street stand flanking the pavement to the left.

Bert Williams trains on the Molineux pitch. The letters in the corner were repeated in the other corner and were for displaying the half-time scores from the other matches taking place, which were listed in the programme.

A full ground watches a match in a different era. No adverts to be seen round the ground, and we know this was Saturday afternoon, because all daylight matches kicked off then at 3 p.m.

Stan Cullis with his 1958 championship winning squad and staff in front of the North Bank with the trophy.

Billy Wright with his England caps and medals and awards. There are only seventy-one caps, so he had another thirty-four to go. Never sent off, never substituted, he played every minute of 105 England games, so that although he is now ninth on the all-time list of England caps, only Peter Shilton (10,725) and Bobby Moore (9,780) have more minutes on the pitch than he does (9,480).

*Left:* Billy Wright with the Championship trophy in 1954. He lifted it three times, as well as the FA Cup. He made 540 appearances for Wolves, plus 112 wartime appearances.

*Below:* Wolves against Arsenal, and the second half has just started as the famous Molineux Clock shows 4 p.m.

Floodlit football, a new dimension to the Molineux experience, made famous by friendly games in the 1950s and later with European competitions.

Billy Wright is applauded off the pitch having retired from the game, having played all his career at Molineux. It was on the occasion of a public practice match in August 1959 at which 20,000 people attended!

Legendary trainer Joe Gardiner
explains something to a young
Ron Flowers who was to carry on
the tradition of Cullis, Wright, and
Slater of captaining Wolves and
playing for England.

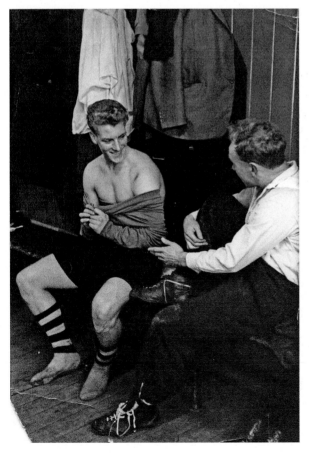

Ron Flowers talks to Billy Wright
in the dressing room. With Eddie
Clamp, they represented a Wolves
and England half back line.

To many supporters, the greatest ever Wolves player, Peter Broadbent, shoots on a snowy pitch under the lights in a European match.

Changes creeping around Molineux in the 1960s. The ring road, to the right, has cut it off from the town centre, with the hotel on its edge. Below that is the short-lived indoor training facility, and the housing to the top left is on borrowed time.

The Molineux from St Peter's Church before the ring road cut through this scene, and before the wholesale market in the foreground was demolished. Also gone are Courtaulds chimneys in the background. All that remains of this scene are Giffard House, in the centre, and Molineux Hotel.

The Wolves bring back the FA Cup in 1960 atop a Don Everall coach at Low Level Station, with Bill Slater and Gerry Harris holding it aloft.

Dawson Street in the 1960s, with the North Bank at the end. Clearly not a match day as there is only one car.

A very different Dawson Street in the 1950s, clearly on a match day.

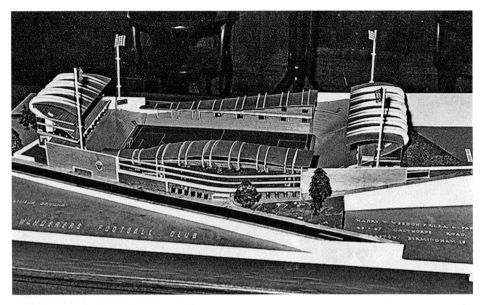

What might have been: the futuristic model of a 70,000-capacity rebuild of the Molineux Stadium mooted around 1960.

Hugh McIllmoyle and Ron Flowers walk out for the second half on a typically muddy pitch in the 1960s, with Peter Knowles just behind them.

*Above:* The queen meets local dignitaries at the Molineux on her visit to the town in 1962.

*Right:* A typical match day programme in the 1960–61 season, which had an unchanged cover for many seasons, and cost only 4*d* (1.5p).

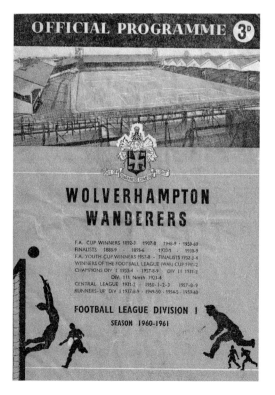

OFFICIAL PROGRAMME 3ᴰ

WOLVERHAMPTON WANDERERS

F.A. CUP WINNERS 1892-3 · 1907-8 · 1948-9 · 1959-60
FINALISTS 1888-9 · 1895-6 · 1920-1 · 1938-9
F.A. YOUTH CUP WINNERS 1957-8 · FINALISTS 1952-3-4
WINNERS OF THE FOOTBALL LEAGUE (WAR) CUP 1941-2
CHAMPIONS DIV 1 1953-4 · 1957-8-9 · DIV II 1931-2
DIV. III North 1923-4
CENTRAL LEAGUE 1931-2 · 1950-1-2-3 · 1957-8-9
RUNNERS-UP DIV I 1937-8-9 · 1949-50 · 1954-5 · 1959-60

FOOTBALL LEAGUE DIVISION I

SEASON 1960-1961

Capt. Mike Bailey receives an award from Chairman John Ireland in 1970.

Bill McGarry's League Cup winning team of 1974.

*Right:* John Richards and Derek Dougan, a strike partnership, with 313 Wolves goals between them, and subsequently Wolves chief executive (Richards) and chairman (Dougan).

*Below:* Oh, the hair! Andy Gray, George Berry, Robert Plant, John Richards, Emyln Hughes, Ken Hibbit, Peter Daniel, and Derek Parkin. Led Zeppelin singer Robert Plant is a lifelong Wolves fan.

Molineux as a heliport. A Queen's Flight Westland Wessex lifts off with the Prince of Wales after a royal visit.

Molineux Street just before it was built on. The buildings to the right were bought by the club and demolished, and the new John Ireland stand was built right behind the old Waterloo Road stand.

Finishing touches being applied to the new stand, the old one having been demolished and turfed over.

Wolves *versus* Manchester City in front of the new stand with Paul Bradshaw, Emyln Hughes, Colin Reeves, Mel Eves, George Berry, and Wayne Clarke

# 5

# Rebirth

In both cases, it was Wolverhampton Council that was to save the day. Derek Dougan, the former Wolves' hero, had resigned his position in January 1985 when it became clear that Allied Properties had no intention of investing in the stadium or the team. In July 1986, the council stepped in and bought the stadium and the adjoining land to the east, the terraced streets between Waterloo Road and North Street. They entered a deal with the construction company Gallagher Bros, who agreed to pay off the club's debt in return for planning permission for an Asda supermarket and car park where the houses had been.

The team started off poorly in the Fourth Division, reaching an embarrassing low in November when they lost to Chorley of the Northern Premier League after a second replay in the first round of the FA Cup. The turning point was at hand, however, when Graham Turner was appointed manager and he bought two players from West Bromwich Albion for a pittance, Andy Thompson and Steve Bull. The team recovered to fourth place but fell to Accrington in the play-offs. Nevertheless, the climb back to respectability had begun, and in 1987–8, Wolves were Fourth Division champions and Sherpa Van Trophy winners at Wembley, where they played in front of 80,000 people. They had become the first club to be champions of all four divisions of the Football League; in fact, five divisions counting both the old Third Division North and the modern Third Division.

Fired by Bull's goals, they were champions again the following year, rising back to the Second Division, though still only having two stands, holding less than 25,000 people. The saviour was at hand, however, when lifelong fan Sir Jack Hayward, born within sight of the ground, bought the club and began redeveloping it, starting with a new stand at the north end, which became the Stan Cullis Stand, and opened in August 1992. The Waterloo Road stand was then demolished and what was named the Billy Wright Stand was built in its stead, opening in 1993, and being followed shortly afterwards by a rebuilt South Bank, named the Jack Harris Stand after a former director.

The community in the shadow of the Molineux had been cleared away and a new Asda supermarket built on the other side of a new road, which was to be named Sir Jack Hayward Way.

Meanwhile, the hotel lay unloved and deteriorating in full view of the passing traffic on the ring road and from the civic centre. In September 2002, the owners sought planning permission to redevelop the building but this was refused, and the following year, arsonists set fire to it. The fierce fire consumed the roof and the interior, and it was something of a miracle that the walls did not crack and fall; building inspectors could not survey the shell except from the outside, it was just too dangerous.

In June 2003, the property companies informed the council that they were going to demolish the buildings as the costs of rebuilding were just too high. The council immediately obtained a court injunction stopping them from carrying this out. With breathing space, the council looked at their options and then decided to acquire the building and to investigate its future use. The need to relocate the City Archives from the former Clarkson's Furniture store building in Snow Hill, which was being redeveloped, offered a solution: the Molineux Hotel would be rebuilt to house the City's Archives.

Once the building was made safe, reconstruction was commenced, using a specialist in the restoration of historic buildings. The decision about how to restore a building that had been added to many times, over a period of two and half centuries, was a difficult one. In the end, the range known as The Manager's House was demolished and a new complimentary extension was built on the western end to house the archives at ideal temperature and humidity. By good fortune, much of the original panelling and fittings had been removed and placed into storage before the fire, when the restoration was originally planned. It was therefore possible to return these to their rightful place. The painstaking work took a great deal of time, and it was not until 10 March 2009 that the building reopened, and the people of Wolverhampton could re-enter and reuse a building that they had come to think of as their own.

Meanwhile, the football club was involved in a roller-coaster ride up and down the divisions. The year 2003 had finally brought promotion to the Premier League via a memorable play-off win in the Millennium Stadium, Cardiff, but they were only to reside there for one season. Relegation was followed by another five seasons in the second tier, now called the Championship, until 2009 when, with Molineux House returned to glory at the top of the hill, the club once more won the Championship Trophy they had last held in 1959, albeit now awarded for winning the 'second division'.

The club had been sold by Sir Jack in 2007 to Steve Morgan for the princely sum of £10, and the promise to invest another £30 million. Expansion of the stadium was begun with the Stan Cullis Stand being demolished in February 2011, replaced with a bigger two-tier structure. The largest end of the Molineux had now moved from the South Bank to the North Bank.

Three years in the top flight was followed by another plummet down two divisions, but thanks to their habit of only ever spending one season at a time in the third tier of English football, they were promoted immediately as champions. Four years treading water were then followed by the Chinese–Portuguese alliance, which took them back to the top table in 2018. The huge Chinese company Fosun bought the club from Steve Morgan in July 2016, and began investing in the team led by a new Portuguese manager, Nuno Espírito Santo, and with many Portuguese players. The Championship Trophy returned in 2018, and the team enjoyed an excellent return to the top flight.

The site of the demolished wholesale market with the Molineux just beyond the new ring road.

Molineux Hotel still open though on the very edge of the ring road, from which there was no direct access.

*Above:* When North Street was cut in half by the ring road, this part was just joined on to Molineux Street. The Feathers is the only building to the right.

*Right:* With two stands closed, Graham Turner directs his team from the scaffolding on the condemned Waterloo Road stand.

*Left:* The Saviour: Steve Bull celebrates one of his 306 goals for the club. It was his goals that restored the team to respectability.

*Below:* When the John Ireland stand was complete, North Street became two cul-de-sacs, this part leading into the Molineux Hotel car park.

The 'Top' Fox, to differentiate it from the Fox Hotel on the Penn Road, and subsequently renamed The Wanderer, lay near the Molineux Hotel, but has now been demolished.

Wolverhampton City Archives, after Molineux House was rebuilt into its third incarnation, with a new archive store added to the left.

The stadium after the Stan Cullis Stand at the north end was enlarged.

The stadium in 2018, with the Asda supermarket and car park where terraced housing used to lie.

The statue of Billy Wright in front of the stand named after him on Waterloo Road, though he still seems to be running away from it, taking his ball with him.

Stan Cullis waves his manager's trilby at fans approaching the stand named after him.

Sir Jack Hayward gives his iconic thumbs up to fans approaching the 'Golden Palace' he built from the tunnel under the ring road. The John Ireland Stand is now renamed the Steve Bull Stand.

*Right:* A fourth Wolves sculpture, a bust of manager Nuno Espírito Santo, created by local ceramic artist Sandra Squires to celebrate the two impressive seasons he inspired.

*Below:* The Molineux Stadium, showing that, on the other side of Waterloo Road at least, terraced housing does still press up against the ground in the manner of traditional football grounds.

In a season that raised the spirits of the whole city, Wolves finished seventh in the league, and performed well against the teams above them. They also reached the semi-final of the FA Cup, narrowly losing to Watford in an exciting match at Wembley. Molineux was full for every match, something that had not happened for many years, and this prompted Fosun to announce further ground expansion. What this all meant to the city was illustrated when Nuno Espírito Santo was awarded a doctorate of sport by the University of Wolverhampton on the pitch before the last game of the season, warmly applauded by over 31,000 fans. Having qualified for European competition once again, the Wolves were set to blaze the name Molineux across the world yet again.